A.E Reed

To order additional copies of this book, contact:
Xlibris
1-888-795-4274
www.Xlibris.com
Orders@Xlibris.com

ISBN: Softcover   978-1-7960-9459-6
       Hardcover   978-1-7960-9460-2
       EBook   978-1-7960-9458-9

Print information available on the last page

Rev. date: 03/17/2020

To my mother
E. T Casanova

To my Father
A. A Reed

Paradise is only a state of mind. It can exist and be wherever you are! For the kingdom resides in your love!

But verily I say unto you... unless your heart can achieve the bliss of a child, you can, in no wise, enter the kingdom!

Welcome...

To

Apple

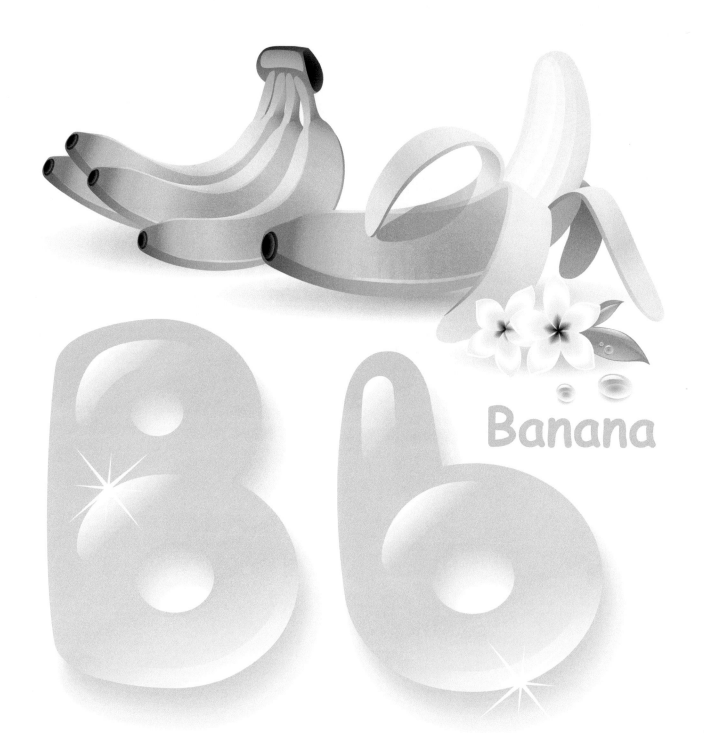

Banana

Bb

Cherry

Dewberry

Dd

Eggplant

Fig

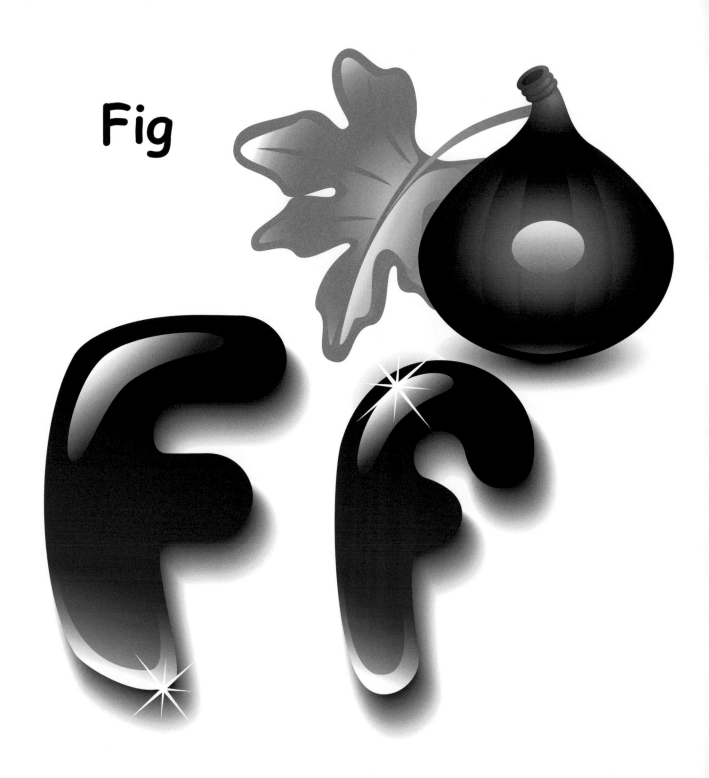

Grapes

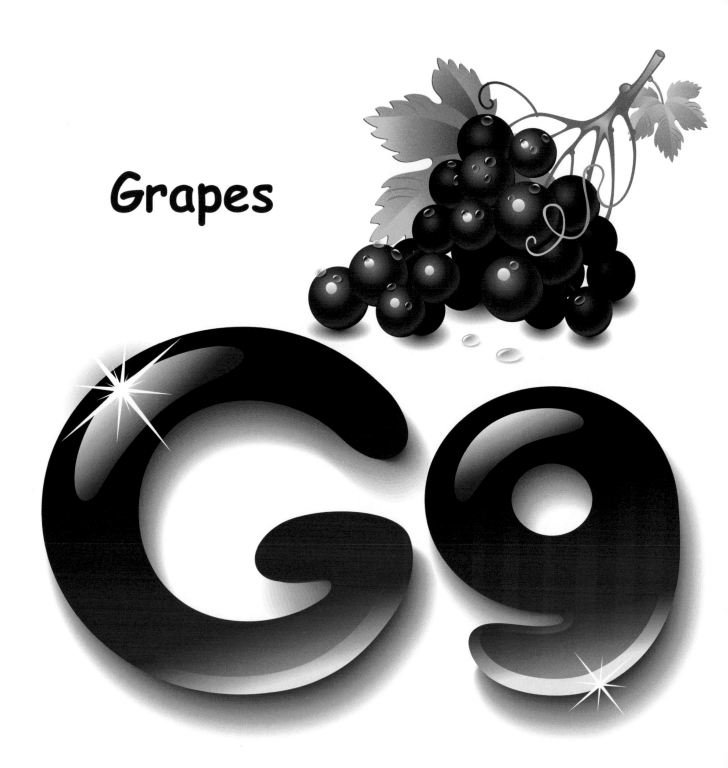

Hazelnuts

Iceberg
lettuce

Jam

Kiwi

Ll

Lemon

Mango

Nectarine

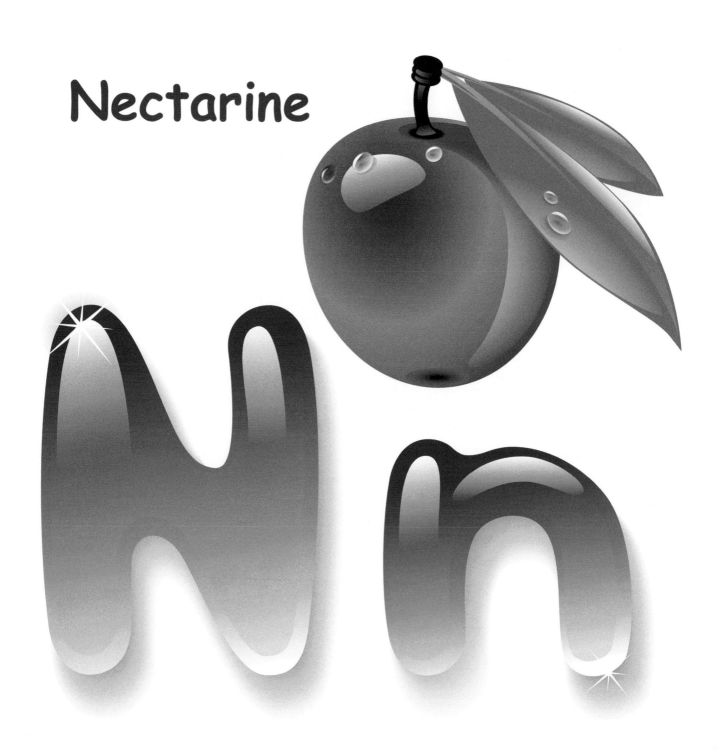

Orange

Plum

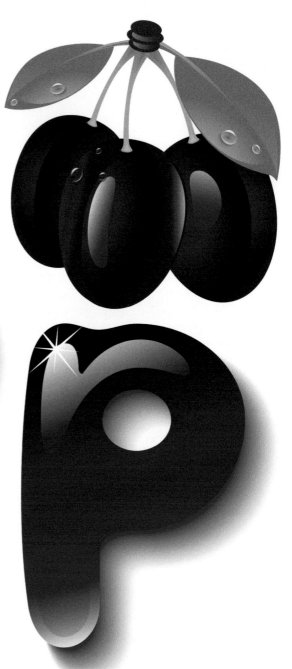

Quince

Raspberry

Strawberry

Tomato

Ugli fruit

Vegetables

Watermelon

Ximenia

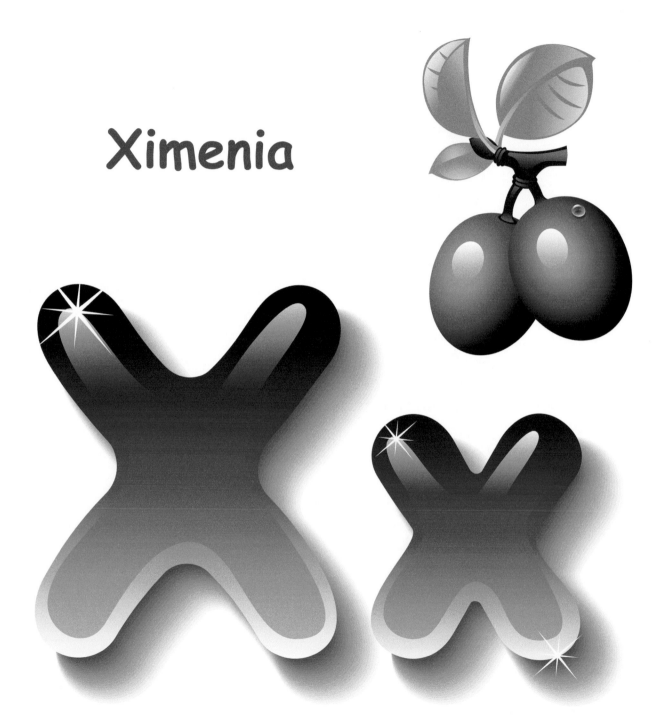

Yellow plum

Y y

Zucchini